The Cotton Patch Version of
Hebrews and the General Epistles

OTHER BOOKS BY CLARENCE JORDAN

The Cotton Patch Version of Paul's Epistles
The Cotton Patch Version of Luke and Acts
The Cotton Patch Version of Matthew and John

EDITED BY DALLAS LEE

The Substance of Faith and Other Cotton Patch
Sermons by Clarence Jordan

The Cotton Patch Version
of Hebrews and
The General Epistles

CLARENCE JORDAN

ASSOCIATION PRESS / NEW YORK

Library of Congress Cataloging in Publication Data

Jordan, Clarence.
The cotton patch version of Hebrews and the general Epistles.

Paraphrased from the Nestle-Aland Greek text, 23d ed., 1957.
1. Bible. N. T. Hebrews—Paraphrases, English. 2. Bible. N. T. Epistles—
Paraphrases, English. I. Title.
BS2773.J67   227'.87'052   73-14856
ISBN 0-8096-1878-8
ISBN 0-8096-1879-6 (pbk.)

PRINTED IN THE UNITED STATES OF AMERICA

CONTENTS

INTRODUCTION

Clarence Jordan arrived in Louisville in the fall of 1933 to enter the Southern Baptist Theological Seminary as a student. I arrived in Louisville in the summer of 1935 to begin in September of that year my work in the Seminary as an instructor in New Testament Interpretation, my chief assignment being the teaching of New Testament Greek.

In those days the Louisville Seminary was among the divinity schools that placed strong emphasis upon the original languages of the Bible—Hebrew and Greek. Both were required for the Master's degree, and this meant for the majority of the students three years of Greek and two of Hebrew. A. T. Robertson, with his "Big Grammar" and many other books, recognized as one of the leading New Testament scholars of the nation, died in 1934, but had left the stamp of his personality and scholarship upon the institution. His successor, W. Hersey Davis, was a master of exegesis and interpretation. Clarence Jordan had the benefit of the scholarship and influence of both these men. It was in this atmosphere he developed a passion to know and interpret the New Testament in the language in which it was written, the *koine* Greek. He determined to become a doctoral student with the Greek New Testament as his major. It was in this way that I came to know him best.

Two very important events happened to Clarence Jordan in 1936. He received his master's degree in theology. And he married Florence Kroeger. She became his true partner in all things. When the dark days came at Koinonia Farm in the fifties, her courage and faithfulness to his ideals were a source of constant inspiration and strength to him.

With her encouragement, Clarence undertook his graduate studies, and so came into ever-deepening contact with the Greek New Testament. Here he began to discover firm theological foundations for the human impulse that was already alive in him. At the same time, he kept that close contact with the problems of practical living which was characteristic of him throughout his life. Not content simply to study, he also became involved in Louisville's teeming inner city and began to see at first hand the fragile life of the poor, who had been driven off the land and who had found only despair in the city.

This involvement in the inner-city life of the black poor led to a teaching position in Simmons University, a black seminary, and later to the directorship of Fellowship Center, supported by the Long Run Baptist Association. Under Clarence's influence Fellowship Center became a focal point of meaningful activities for underprivileged black adults and children, and a center of fellowship between black and white Baptists. It also afforded an opportunity for Seminary students to become involved in practical social Christianity. Clarence must have discharged his responsibilities well, for he was asked to become the first "full-time" superintendent of missions of the Long Run Association. Somehow, amidst all the extracurricular activities he engaged in, Clarence managed to keep up his doctoral work at the Seminary and in 1939 received his doctor's degree in Greek New Testament.

It was during this same period that the idea of *Koinonia* began to germinate in Clarence's mind. The story in Acts 2:43–47 and 4:32–37 of the communal life of the early disciples became a sort of magnet that drew his thoughts to the possibilities of this primitive expression of Christian love and sharing in modern life. He drew around him a small group of Seminary students and formed a fellowship that sought to imitate the primitive Christian community in the practice of "holding all things in common." This was the first practical projection of what was to develop in south Georgia as the nationally known Koinonia Farm. More and more as time drew on, Clarence was turning his eyes southward and was dreaming of the establishment in the Deep South of an experiment in practical Christian love that would demonstrate to the world that whites and blacks could live and work side by side in sharing a common enterprise. The details of this amazing story have been told many times, and need not be repeated here.

After Clarence left Louisville I did not have many personal contacts with him, but I was aware of the suspicion Koinonia Farm aroused in the surrounding community, a suspicion that grew into hate, abuse and violence. However, his rejection in the South resulted in openings for speaking engagements in other parts of the nation and gave Koinonia a nationwide hearing. Before he died in 1969 Clarence was invited to speak at Southern, his old seminary, and at Southeastern Baptist Seminary at Wake Forest, North Carolina. Things do change!

Looking back, it now seems almost inevitable that from this effort to live out the meaning of New Testament love in the cotton fields of south Georgia, Clarence should have begun a translation which would eventually give the world "the Cotton Patch Version" of the New Testament. By education and by dedication, he was uniquely qualified for the task. It started as he would make his own translation of a scriptural passage he wanted to use in preaching. Only gradually did he realize he had hit upon a style of translation that brought the Word to the reader with a new contemporary power. As time went by, he completed individual books of the New Testament which were widely circulated in pamphlet form. But eventually he had done enough to be able to publish *The Cotton Patch Version of Paul's Epistles*.

When I received from Clarence Jordan in February of 1968 an autographed copy of that book, I recognized that he had accomplished something unique in the history of Biblical interpretation. As he wrote in his Introduction, he had "made an attempt to translate not only the words but the events." He possessed the genius to be able to change the biblical setting from first-century Palestine to twentieth-century America, and to transport the biblical characters across the time-space barrier so that they not only spoke modern English, but talked about modern problems, feelings, frustrations, hopes and assurances. It was as though they worked beside the reader in the cotton patch or on the assembly line, so that the Word became modern *flesh*.

Above all else, the "cotton patch version" is a projection of the life and character of Clarence Jordan himself. He was a combination of the erudite scholar and the bold man of action. In the truest sense of the word he was a prophet—one who spoke forth for God. In the expression of his convictions he was straightforward and sometimes his language was shocking to modern ears. This was true of his preaching—which was direct, and Bible-centered, and sternly contemporary—as well as his translation of the New Testament into the "cotton patch version." For he spoke with the earthiness of Amos of Tekoa, the boldness of Jeremiah, but often with the tenderness of Hosea. There was something in Clarence of the asceticism and gentleness of Saint Francis of Assisi but he never deserted the contemporary scene and spoke and wrote with the dogged determination of Martin Luther.

Clarence did not claim that his "cotton patch" version always represented a literal rendition of the Greek text. He did not call his work a translation but a "version." This gave him the liberty he desired to give a distinctly contemporary color and flavor to the gospel story as recorded in the pages of the New Testament. The result has the effect of shocking some readers, amusing others, but winning the nod of approval of many.

Clarence Jordan died unexpectedly on October 29, 1969, at the age of fifty-seven. At the time of his death, there were some few parts of the New Testament which he had not yet translated. The task might never have been finished. Clarence himself doubted that it would be possible successfully to "cotton patch" the book of Revelation. The other portions which remained undone were the Gospel of Mark and several chapters of the Gospel of John. With these exceptions, the entire New Testament is now available in the Cotton Patch Version.

The same daring contemporary language and applications will be found throughout. The only way for the reader to appreciate what Clarence Jordan has done is to read for himself the letters, Gospels and Acts as he has given them to us. Let the reader discover for himself the bold and stimulating efforts one of God's true prophets has made to make the New Testament come alive in a time when the world needs as never before the Living Word.

EDWARD A. McDOWELL, JR.

Translator's Notes

The letter to the Hebrews is actually a sermon to Jewish converts to Christianity. Its purpose is to help them understand their newly found faith in Christ and his Movement, so that they might be intelligent, faithful and zealous members of the fellowship.

Perhaps it was the convention sermon at an Annual Conference of early Christians. The delegates may have been so impressed and so inspired that they insisted it be included in the Convention minutes. Just who the learned and eloquent preacher was, we do not know. One thing is certain—it was not Paul. My guess is that it was Apollos, for the description of him given in Acts 18:24-28 perfectly fits the requirements for the author of this lecture.

The letter of James, a rather rambling sermon, bristles with similarities to Jesus' great Lesson on the Mount. It, too, calls for the practical application of the faith by turning belief into action.

The so-called "general epistles" come from some of the earliest partners in the faith of Jesus Christ and sparkle with keen insight and spiritual perception. They abound in compassion, love, encouragement and hope. With fiery zeal they warn us of the perils of indifference and lukewarmness, and of the tribulations which invariably befall the faithful. And we have the feeling that these partners were speaking out of their own experiences of love, joy and suffering.

Rock would remind us that Christians are a special breed of people, clearly distinguishable from those ruled by the world spirit. Jack pleads for that tough love which expresses itself in genuine concern for one's brother. And Joe would have us keep a sharp eye on those who would twist the faith out of shape.

CLARENCE JORDAN

Publisher's Note: These comments were written by Clarence Jordan for the individual booklets in which these New Testament translations first appeared. They have been collected and reprinted here in slightly edited form because they represent the best statement of the meaning Clarence had found in this material, and the way he understood it.

THE LETTER
TO THE HEBREWS
A first-century manual for church renewal

CHAPTER 1

1. In the past God spoke to men at different times and in all kinds of ways through prophets, but just recently he has spoken to us through a son, whom he appointed overseer of everything and through whom God made history. He is a clear reflection of God, and he makes it easy to understand his character. Moreover, he supports it all with powerfully convincing evidence.

4. When he had made a clean sweep of wickedness, he assumed his place as leader, under God, of the powerful and exalted spiritual forces. He is as far above the angels as his title, Son, indicates. For to what angel has God ever said,

> "You are my son, I myself sired you"
>
> or
>
> "I shall be like a father to him,
> And he shall be like a son to me"?

And again, in bringing his first-born into the world, he says:

> "Let all God's angels kneel before him."

Regarding angels he says:

> "He makes his angels breezes,
> And his ministers flames of fire."

But about his son he says:

> "Your divine throne is everlasting,
> And your royal rule is benevolent,
> For you loved right and hated wrong.
> Therefore God—your God—has inaugurated you
> Into an office above that of any of your contemporaries."

He also says:

> "You, O Lord, laid out the foundations of the world
>   at the beginning;
> And the skies are all your handwork.
> While they perish, you persist;
> They shall all wear out like an old shoe,
> And you will roll them up like a shirt, and trade them in.
> But with you it's different; you're aways the same,
> And the years leave no mark on you."

Now to what angel has he ever said:

> "You be my 'right hand man',
>   While I put all other contenders
>   Under your official sway."?

Really, aren't angels simply spiritual "altar boys," sent out to do what they can to help those sincerely seeking salvation?

CHAPTER 2

1. Now please, let's pay much more attention to what we've heard, and let's not let our minds wander. For if the sermons of God's messengers proved true, and every sin and crime denounced by them was justly punished, how do you think we'll escape if we disregard the kind of salvation which, to begin with, was explained by the Lord and then confirmed to us by those who actually heard him? And especially since God himself backed it all up with signs and wonders and all kinds of miracles, and even the sending of the Holy Spirit whenever he chose.

5. Now God hasn't put this whole new order that we're dis-

20

cussing in the hands of angels. Somewhere there's a Scripture like this:

> "Who is man, that you should notice him,
> Or man's child, that you should take an interest in him?
> Only for a time you made him lower than the angels;
> Then you elevated him to a position of honor and trust,
> And turned everything over to him."

When we speak of "turning everything over," nothing is excluded. Of course, at present we don't see this as an accomplished fact. But I do think that the sentence, "Only for a time you made him lower than the angels," refers to Jesus who, because he made the supreme sacrifice, was elevated to a position of honor and trust, so that he, by God's grace, might taste of death for each of us.

10. For even though he has ultimate authority over everything and everybody, it was nothing but right that he, as the head of a remarkable deliverance movement, should take the lead among his many followers in going all the way in suffering the cause. For he who calls *for* commitment, and they who respond *with* commitment are all together in the same boat. That's why he isn't ashamed to identify himself with them as his brothers. To quote another Scripture:

> "I will tell my brothers your name,
> I'll join with them in congregational singing."

And in another place:

> "I shall put the utmost confidence in him."

And still again:

"Here I am with the dedicated band which God has given me."

14. Since the "dedicated band" were frail mortals, he himself became one, too, so that by dying he might break the grip of the one who controls death—that is, the devil—and set free those people who, all their lives, have been dominated by a fear of death. It is as clear as day that his real concern is not with angels, but with plain ordinary human beings. That's why he became just like one of "the brethren," and is such a gracious and dedicated spiritual leader. He is completely devoted to God's work and able to deal effectively with the sins of his followers. Since he himself has been tempted and has suffered so deeply, he knows how to sympathize fully with those who also are being tempted.

CHAPTER 3

1. So then, committed brothers, partners in the spiritual assignment, give careful consideration to Jesus, the founder and leader of our movement. For he was loyal to the one who appointed him, just as Moses was a loyal leader of his people. But Jesus is as much greater than Moses, as the architect is greater than the house he designs. While every house is designed by someone, God alone is the master architect. Now Moses was indeed a trustworthy leader of his people as a *deputy*, a symbol of the things to be explained later. On the other hand, Christ leads his people not as the King's deputy but as his own *son*. And we Christians are his people, provided of course that to the very last detail, we diligently carry through on our courage and our confidence in our only hope. It's just like the Holy Spirit says:

"If you would take him seriously today,
    Don't let your souls get calloused, like they did that day in
        the wilderness,
    When I got sick and tired of their demands for 'proof';

When your fathers tried my patience with their 'let's-be-
practical' speeches,
And were given forty years in which to see plenty of my
'proof.'
So I got thoroughly fed up with that bunch and I said,
'They are eternally making a mess of things
Simply because they pay no attention to my instructions.'
While in this up-set condition I swore
That they would *never* achieve my rest."

12. Take extreme care, brothers, to see that not a one of you
might have such a wicked and untrustful attitude as to turn your
back on the living God. Rather, remind each other every day
during this period we call "today," or "the present," not to let
one's soul get calloused by flimsy excuses. For we are Christ's
partners only if we steadfastly carry through on our commitment
from beginning to end, just like it says:

"If you would take him seriously today,
Don't let your souls get calloused like they did that day
in the wilderness."

16. Let me ask you, who were the ones who were still stubborn even after they heard the full report? Wasn't it practically
the whole gang that came out of Egypt under Moses? And with
whom did God get fed up for those forty years? Wasn't it with
those who missed the mark and who died like flies in the wilderness? And wasn't it to the distrustful that he swore that they
would never arrive at his destination? So it is obvious that it was
lack of faith that kept them from making the grade.

CHAPTER 4

1. Therefore it should really frighten us to realize that we,

23

like them, are given an opportunity to enter his "Promised Land," with the same possibility also that some of us might flub-the-dub. For we have had the good news (that God has a kingdom prepared for his people) to fall on our ears the same as they. The reason it didn't do them one bit of good was because their hearing and their behavior didn't connect. For only they who act on their convictions enter the "Sabbath," just as it says:

> "While in this up-set condition I swore
> That they would never achieve my rest."

He speaks of his "rest" even though work has been continuing since creation. Somewhere there's a reference to the seventh day like this: "And God entered on the seventh day into a state of rest from all his works." And then again, "They shall not enter my state of rest." Since it is implied that some will enter it, and since those who were originally told about the promised land didn't make the grade because they didn't live by the Unseen, God has decided to provide another opportunity which he calls "To-day" or "Now," just as he says later in one of David's psalms:

> "Today if you are serious about following him
> Don't let your souls get calloused."

8. For if, under Joshua, they had achieved God's rest, then God wouldn't have spoken of still another day. You see, then, that a "Sabbatism" has been saved for God's people. For he who finally achieves his "rest," or goal, need no longer struggle. It's like God did when he wound up creation.

11. Therefore, let's put everything we've got into entering that "rest," so that none of us will fall into the same trap as those who wouldn't trust him. For God's word is alive with energy, and sharper than any double-edged sword you ever saw; so sharp, in fact, that it can draw a line between the mental and the spiritual, like separating bones from marrow, and discern all our inner emotions and drives. For there isn't a thing in the world he doesn't notice. Before him, whose word searches us, everything stands naked and bare.

14. Since we have such a great, heaven-sent spiritual leader as Jesus, God's son, let's get on the ball. For we have a leader who isn't coldly indifferent to our weaknesses, but who himself has been put through the mill like we have, yet without giving in. So let's hold our heads high as we pass his "reviewing stand," having every assurance that we shall both find and be given all the mercy and inner strength we need for any situation.

CHAPTER 5

1. One of the qualifications of a spiritual leader of men is his ability to interpret God to them and to help them have a sense of his presence and forgiveness. In addition, he has a tender spot in hs heart for the uneducated and the fallen, since he knows that he himself is a weak human being. That's why, in seeking God's forgiveness for his people, he must also seek it for himself. And a man does not appoint himself to such a sacred task—it is a call from God, like Aaron's.

5. So Christ didn't just up and appoint himself a spiritual leader. God did it when he said to him:

"You are my son; today I fathered you."

And in another place he says:

"You are an immortal spiritual leader, a sort of 'Melchisedec.' "

During those days when Jesus was a man, he agonized in prayer, sometimes with pained outcries and tears, pouring out his heart to the one who could have saved him from such a death. And God listened to this kind of devout sincerity. Even though Jesus was a son, he learned his leasson the hard way. And when he had matured, he became an inspiring example of spiritual emancipation to those who come under his discipline, having been approved by God as "a spiritual leader, a sort of Melchisedec."

There's a lot I'd like to say about this, but it's so hard to explain to people with limited understanding. You all have had plenty of time to be teachers by now, and yet you still need somebody to teach you the kindergarten stuff of the Gospel! In fact, you're still on the bottle and can't take solid food. The fellow who is still on the bottle isn't a seasoned veteran in the good cause—he's just a kid! Solid food is for adults who, by strenuous exercise, have sharpened their abilities to distinguish between good and bad.

CHAPTER 6

1. So then let's move on from the basic Christian teachings to the more mature things of the faith. For it shouldn't be necessary to discuss again such topics as "Turning Away from Empty Observances," "Faith in God," "The Doctrine of Baptism," "The Laying On of Hands," "Resurrection of the Dead," and "Hellfire and Damnation." God permitting, we'll go on to other matters.

Once a man has seen the light and has had a good taste of truly spiritual food and has become one of the Holy Spirit's partners and has chewed on God's good word and has felt the vibrant power of the coming revolution, and then gives up the struggle, it is hopeless ever to get him to try again. Inwardly he re-crucifies the Son of God and holds him in contempt. For example, land which has drunk in the rains and has produced abundant crops for the farmer is highly cherished. But if it won't grow anything but weeds and briars, it is unloved, cussed at, and burned over.

26

THE LETTER TO THE HEBREWS

9. Even though we're talking like this, we do have a high regard for you in the coming regime. For God is not so inconsiderate as to forget the good you've done and the love you have displayed for his cause as you have served—and still are serving—the members of the fellowship. We surely hope that each of you will show the same diligence in carrying through on the goal to its full accomplishment. Don't be spiritual morons; rather, be imitators of those great souls who by creative and persistent effort achieved their dreams.

13. Take a man like Abraham, to whom God promised: "I'm going to bless you and make your family reunions crowded." He won this promise by his sheer tenacity. (Actually, it was more of a pledge, or oath, than promise, and since God had no one above him to administer an oath, he swore on his own. Men take their oaths under a higher authority, and in every dispute their oath becomes the point upon which truth is established. So when God wanted to make all the more clear to his followers that he wouldn't let them down, he made it binding with an oath.) Because of two absolutely certain things—the oath, plus the fact that God can't lie anyway—we "refugees" can find strong encouragement to take hold of the hope held out to us. Such hope is like an anchor for our souls, to steady us and keep us safe. And its roots lie deep in the beginnings of our faith when Jesus, like a pioneer, blazed a trail for us and became our spiritual leader, "a sort of Melchisedec."

CHAPTER 7

1. Now this Melchisedec, King of Peace, was God Almighty's preacher. He met Abraham coming back from the butchering of the royalty, and praised him. Whereupon, Abraham gave him a tenth of the loot. (When you translate this man's title it means a

"King of Righteousness," or more literally, "King of Peace," which more accurately translates King of "Salem.") Fatherless, motherless, without any kinfolk, having neither birth certificate nor record of his death, he is like the Son of God a timeless, eternally contemporary preacher.

Just think of it! He was such a great guy that Abraham the Patriarch gave him a tenth of his very best loot! Now clergymen have a church rule to accept tithes, in God's name, from their people, their own brothers and sisters, even though there's no distinction between clergy and laity. But Melchisedec, *who is in no way related to the clergy,* accepted tithes from Abraham and blessed him, a man himself of great spiritual maturity. Beyond any doubt the little man is always blessed by the one higher up. And on the one hand tithes are received by frail humans, while on the other they are received by one who is eternally alive. We might even say that in a sense the clergy themselves paid tithes through Abraham, since they were his unborn descendants at the time Melchisedec met him.

11. Now if one could become spiritually mature merely by entering the ministry (an honorable profession through which the people are spiritually nourished), why should there still be a need for a radically different type of minister (the Melchisedec kind), rather than the average, typical parson? When a change is made in the kind of preacher, there will also of necessity be a change in the type of message.

13. The one we're talking about is entirely different from the usual clergyman. He was no professional at all. For it is perfectly obvious that our Lord was a layman. He doesn't therefore come under the usual "ordination" procedures. The difference is all the more obvious when there arises a radically different minister (the Melchisedec type), who doesn't follow the traditional social patterns but whose power stems from his uncompromising stand. And this is true of Jesus, just as it says,

"You are an eternally contemporary minister of the Melchisedec type."

Clearly, then, there is a change in the traditional approach, which has always been weak and ineffective (custom never made a saint out of anybody), and a much better way has been ushered in. By it we come into God's presence.

So we can't say that Jesus was without divine approval, like some self-styled preachers who have set *themselves* up in business. God himself "ordained" Jesus when he said to him, "The Lord, who never retracts, has pledged, 'You are an eternally contemporary minister.' " This makes Jesus the founder of a vastly superior order.

23. Also, there is a continuous procession of human clergymen, because death prevents them from staying in office indefinitely. But he, the eternal contemporary, has an ageless ministry. That's why he is forever able to save those who approach God through him—he's always on the alert to assist them in every way possible. He's the man for us—a qualified spiritual leader, dedicated, sincere, incorruptible, having no truck with hoodlums, a highminded man out of this world. It isn't necessary for him, like other ministers, to go through all the rigamarole of daily masses, worship services, etc. He got all that over with once and for all when he offered up himself. By tradition, frail humans are ordained into the ministry, but God's solemn vow, which supersedes tradition, has ordained the stalwart Son, the Eternal Contemporary.

CHAPTER 8

1. In substance, what we're saying is that we have an outstanding spiritual leader who is at the top of God Almighty's list. He is pastor of the true church established by the Lord, not by man. Every minister is ordained to conduct worship services and take up offerings, so he himself certainly should set the example in these things. But if Jesus were on earth, he probably wouldn't be a preacher at all, since there are plenty of parsons to conduct traditional worship services. Their meetings are only a type or symbol of the true, spiritual gatherings. It's somewhat like God's warning when Moses was about to begin his building program: "See to it," he said, "that you build everything according to the model which was shown you on the mountain."

Now Jesus has set up worship services which are deeply meaningful, since he is the author of a more vital commitment, or constitution, which is based upon vastly superior ideas. For if that first commitment, or constitution, had been successful, there would have been no need to draw up a second. But God brands the first a failure when he says,

"The days are coming," says the Lord, "when I will draw up a new constitution for the Jewish nation—not the kind I made with their founding fathers when I took them by the hand and led them out of Egypt. They wouldn't live by that constitution, so I walked out on them," says the Lord. "This constitution which I shall propose for the future Jewish nation," says the Lord, "will be an inner one in which my principles will be imbedded in their minds and hearts. And I shall be 'God-in-them' and they shall be a 'nation-in-me.' And not a single one of them will need to teach his fellow citizen or his brother, saying, 'Here's the way to know the Lord.' For everybody, from the little fellow to the high brass, will already know me. And I will be patient with their shortcomings, and I won't ever throw their sins in their faces."

Note that when mention is made of "the new constitution" it makes the first constitution an old one. And anything that's old and worn out is headed for the garbage can.

CHAPTER 9

1. The first constitution spelled out the order of worship and the arrangement of the sanctuary. The outer room, which is called "Holy," was fixed up with a lampstand and a table and a place for receiving the bread. Beyond the second curtain was another sanctuary called "Holy of Holies," in which was a gold altar and the constitution's gold-covered showcase. In the showcase were a gold jar containing a sample of the manna, and Aaron's stick that sprouted, and the original copy of the constitution. Above this were the gorgeous cherubim hovering over the Forgiveness exhibit. There's no need now to go into further detail about these things. When everything is in order, the priests are constantly on duty in the outer sanctuary performing their liturgical services. But only the high priest is allowed into the inner sanctuary, and he but once a year. On this occasion he must take blood to offer for the stupid acts of both himself and the people. This is sort of a parable or symbol pointing to the present situation by which the Holy Spirit makes it clear that unimpeded access to the Holy of Holies is not possible so long as the outer sanctuary is still in existence with its gifts and sacrifices. These things cannot develop the inner life of the worshipper since they are externals —bread and wine and holy water—mere physical symbols pointing to spiritual truths.

11. When Christ came, however, he was a minister of more meaningful things in a vastly better and more advanced sanctuary which was not built by human hands and cannot, therefore, be claimed as a human achievement. Nor did he go through all that goat-and-calf-blood ritual. Instead he made himself expendable and entered once for all into the "Holy Place" and made the supreme sacrifice for our lasting welfare. For if you think that the ritual of sprinkling the blood of goats and bulls and the ashes of a heifer has a cleansing effect on the bodies of those who consider themselves ceremonially defiled, how much more will Christ's supreme sacrifice, which he made in a spiritual way by offering himself to God without reservation, effectively cleanse our consciences from dead rules so we can worship the living God.

31

15. Furthermore, he is the administrator of a new will. And now that a death has occurred and a release obtained from the excessive demands of the first will, the participants may share in the provisions of the spiritual inheritance. (In the case of a will, it is necessary, you know, to prove the death of the one making it.) A will is for the establishment of the rights of the dead, since it does not go into effect while the person is still living. This is why the previous will couldn't have become effective without blood, a symbol of a death. You recall that when Moses had explained each commandment of the constitution, he took the blood of fattened calves and goats, mixed it with water and strands of red wool and spice, and then sprinkled it on both the document and the people. As he did so he said,

"This is the blood of the will which God drew up for you."

He also sprinkled the blood on the sanctuary and on all things used during the worship services. In fact, legally speaking, almost everything requires blood to clear it. So that without some kind of blood-shedding, there is no contract. If, then, it is necessary for the earthly symbols of spiritual things to be cleansed, the actual spiritual things themselves require a still more effective sacrifice. For Christ didn't enter any humanly designed temples, which merely symbolize the real one. Rather, he entered the spiritual realm itself, where he now represents us before God. It isn't necessary, either, that he repeat his sacrifice, like the high priest does each year when he enters the Temple with blood which is not his own. If this were required, then Jesus would have to go through his sufferings over and over again from the beginning of time. But now at this high point of history, he has come on the scene and nullified sin by his one complete sacrifice. And just as it is required that men die only once and then face the judgment, so Christ also, having been already offered in one final act to bear everybody's sin, will hereafter be related to his eager associates not from the standpoint of sin but of spiritual growth.

CHAPTER 10

1. At best, the old set of rules and regulations merely foreshadowed the coming Reality. It was never the genuine article itself. That's why it was incapable of bringing spiritual maturity to the congregation by its round of annual sacrifices. If it could have, the need for such sacrifices would have by now ceased to exist. For once you get a congregation genuinely forgiven of its sins, it no longer has a guilty conscience about them. Yet under the old system they are told, at the annual sacrifice, that they are guilty sinners. Evidently, the blood of cattle and goats just can't take away sins!

5. So when He came into the world, he agreed with the Psalmist:

"You don't want the outward sacrifice, the showy giving;
Rather, you have woven me into a fellowship.
You were never pleased with the elaborate displays,
And the shallow confessions of sin.
Then I respond, 'O God, I have come *to do your will*.'
And He said, 'Every chapter in the Bible is about Me.' "

8. When it says that "you neither wanted nor were pleased with the external sacrifice, the showy giving, the elaborate displays and the shallow confessions," he was referring to the things laid down in the old set of rules and regulations. Then he continues, "I have come *to do your will*." Thus he abandons the former that he might concentrate on the latter. And what is his will? That we should be a people set apart by the one final offering of the Body of Jesus Christ.

11. Another thing: Every minister gets up and in his liturgy for the day goes through the same thing over and over. All of which has no power to get people out of their sins. But this minister made one final sweep of sin by his supreme sacrifice and then took his place by God's side as his "right arm," with the confident expectation of ultimate victory. By this one act of self-giving he has fully outfitted for all time those who are dedicated to the cause. The Holy Spirit also confirms this when he says:

"This constitution which I shall draw up for them—the time will come," says the Lord, "when I will lay my laws on their hearts and I will burn them into their minds. Then I can forget all about their sinful conduct and lawless behavior." So, where there is an effective handling of such sinful conduct, there need be no further means of eliminating it.

19. So then, brothers, let us draw courage, from Jesus' supreme sacrifice, to enter the "sanctuary." For by breaking through "this veil of clay," he opened up for us a meaningful and vital way of life. And with a Great Spiritual Leader over God's movement, let's keep walking with a pure motive and an abundance of faith. Let's cleanse our hearts from any unworthy feeling and let's bathe our group in clean water. Let us hang on with tooth and toenail to our promising commitment, for he who maps our strategy can be completely trusted. And let's think up ways to provoke everybody into "fits of love and kindness." Don't fail to meet together in cell groups, as some are beginning to do. Rather, keep everybody on his toes, especially as you see D-day approaching.

For, if we keep on deliberately sinning after the truth has been clearly explained to us, there is no further means of dealing with our sin. Such a person can expect the awful judgment and the roaring flame which waits to consume the stubborn.

When a man broke a law of Moses, and it was proved by as many as two or three witnesses, he was given the death sentence without mercy. Don't you think a much worse punishment is deserved by the man who runs roughshod over the son of God, and who considers the bloodstained constitution, to which he owes his citizenship, a mere scrap of paper, and who pokes fun at the spirit of self-giving? For we know who's talking when it says:

"Execution of the sentence is up to me; I will see that justice is done."

And again:

"The Lord will have final say-so over his people."

How frightening it is to be delivered into the custody of God Almighty!!

32. Always remember the early days of your conversion when you went through a great struggle that caused you much suffering. Sometimes a mob would gather and cuss you out and beat you up. At other times you caught it because you stood up for those who were living this way. You all suffered together with those who went to jail, and you accepted with joy the seizure of your property. You knew that you had a more precious and lasting Possession. Just don't squander your prize which can pay you handsome dividends. You need a lot of determination to carry through on the will of God and hit the jackpot.

> "By and by, sooner than you think
> The Leader will arrive, and he won't go slow.
> And my dedicated man shall live his faith;
> But if he chickens out, I'll be ashamed of him."

We are not cowards doomed to failure, but men of faith finding meaning to life!

CHAPTER 11

1. Now faith is the turning of dreams into deeds; it is betting your life on the unseen realities. It was for such faith that men of old were martyred. And by so relating our lives, we become aware that history is woven to God's design, so that the seen event is a projection of the Unseen Intent.

Living by the Unseen, Abel brought to God a more acceptable sacrifice than Cain. By so living he got the O.K. for being on the right track, as evidenced by the fact that God approved his gifts. Such a life, though snuffed out, is still speaking.

Living by the Unseen, Enoch was transfigured so that he didn't die. His corpse was never found, because God transfigured him. Without living by the Unseen, it's impossible to get such approval. For anyone who is serious about the God-life, must stake everything on the fact that God is, and that he amply rewards those who make him their quest.

Living by the Unseen, Abraham obeyed when he was called upon to depart for a country which was going to be his inheritance. And he set out without knowing where he was heading.

Living by the Unseen, he homesteaded in the Promised Land like a foreigner, living in temporary shelters with Isaac and Jacob, who had inherited with him the same mission. For he had his heart set on a permanent city, whose architect and general contractor is God.

Living by the Unseen, Sarah herself had a full-term pregnancy, even though she had passed her menopause. She was sure all along that God would carry through on what he had promised. So it was through her that one man, practically dead, sired descendants as countless as the stars in the sky and as numberless as grains of sand on the ocean beach.

13. Holding fast to their life by the Unseen, these all died without experiencing the final outcome. But they did see it from a distance and cheered for it. They frankly admitted that they themselves were aliens and transients in society. (People who talk in this way are actually referring to the fact that they have their heart set on a land they can call "home." If they were really attached to their birthplace, they would have plenty of chances to return to it. But as it is, they are yearning for a better land—that is, a spiritual one.) Therefore God was not embarrassed to have them call him God. In fact, he had a community all ready for them.

17. Living by the Unseen, Abraham, when he was put to the test, offered up Isaac. The man who had been let in on the "Grand Design" laid on the altar his only son, the one to whom God referred when he said, "Your descendants will come through Isaac." He was convinced that God could raise him from the dead if need be. So, figuratively speaking, Abraham did get him back from the dead.

Living by the Unseen, Isaac gave Jacob and Esau blessings which were yet to be realized.

Living by the Unseen, Jacob, on the day he died, blessed each of Joseph's sons while he reverently leaned on the handle of his cane.

Living by the Unseen, Joseph, before his death, saw the Exodus of the Israelites coming, and gave instructions about his remains.

Living by the Unseen, the parents of Moses hid him for three months after he was born. They recognized that he was an unusual child, and were not intimidated by the King's decree. Living by the Unseen, Moses himself, when he had become a great man, refused to be called a son of the Emperor's daughter. Rather, he chose to identify himself with God's people in their oppression than to have the temporary comforts of a life of ease. He figured that the hardship of the Christlike life was worth a lot more than the luxuries of Egypt. He had an eye for real values.

27. Living by the Unseen, he *walked* out of Egypt; he didn't *run* from the wrath of the king. Like a man who sees the Unseen, he pressed on. Living by the Unseen, he provided for the sprinkling of blood at the Passover so the Slayer of the First-Born might not harm the Israelites. Living by the Unseen, they went through the Red Sea like it was dry ground. When the Egyptians made a try at it they were swallowed up. Living by the Unseen; they toppled the walls of Jericho after seven days of marching around them. Living by the Unseen, the whore Rahab escaped the destruction of the wayward by befriending our intelligence agents.

And what more shall I say? Time would run out on me if I told about Gideon, Barak, Samson, Jephtha, David, Samuel and the prophets. Living by the Unseen, all of these went to war against kingdoms, carried the banner of civilization, obtained treaties, muzzled lions' mouths, smothered fires, escaped from death by the sword, got their second wind when they had given out, became highly successful in war, and overcame foreign armies. Wives whose husbands were reported dead got them back alive. Some people were tortured terribly when they refused bail in order to make a better witness. Still others took a lot of abuse and beatings, and repeated arrests and jailings. Rocks were thrown at them, they were investigated, they were hacked apart and butchered with swords, they wore rags and cast-off clothing—wretchedly poor, hounded, treated disgracefully (people too honorable for the world), herded into slums and tenements and hovels and even holes in the ground.

39. That all of these lived by the Unseen is well-documented. Yet they did not participate in the final outcome, because God had in mind something better which involved us, too, so that neither they nor us could be complete without each other.

CHAPTER 12

1. Now here's where we come in. Surrounded by such a cloud of veterans of the faith, let's strip off all heavy and tight-fitting clothes * and run with endurance the race stretching out before

---

* The Greek words for "sin" and "cloak" are phonetically almost identical. I believe that the scribe who copied this manuscript mistakenly wrote "sin" (as in RSV) instead of "cloak," as I have translated it.

us. Let's keep our eyes fixed on Jesus, the founder and guiding spirit of our way of life. In place of joy that stretched out before him, he took on a cross, without hesitating one second to consider the disgrace involved. Now he is God's "righthand man." So take another look at him who put up with so much opposition from "the good-people-of-this-town." It'll keep you from getting blue and down in the dumps. After all, *you* haven't stood up to the point of shedding any of *your* blood in the struggle against sin. Perhaps you should recall the passage which refers to you as "sons":

"My son, don't minimize the value of a celestial spanking,
    And don't let it get you down when you're bawled out
        from on high.
    For the Lord has got to love you to spank you,
    And he uses the belt on only a son."

7. Take your "spanking" like a man—it is evidence that God regards you as *sons*. For what son is there with a father who never spanks him? If you're without your spanking, which all the other boys got, then you must be bastards and not true sons. Clearly we have great respect for our human fathers when they spank us. Then how much more should we put ourselves under the spiritual Father and prepare for life. For *they* spanked us for a limited period and at their own discretion, but *he* does it for our welfare to help us dare to be different for him. Indeed, every spanking, while it is going on, is not a joy but a grief. But afterwards it shows up in the peaceful and upright lives of those whose rear ends were so exercised. Therefore, get some pep into your sagging hands and shaking bones. Give your feet a good workout, so they'll stay in good shape and not develop fallen arches.

Go all out for peace with everyone, and for the different life, without which nobody can get to first base with the Lord. Coach a member to keep him from flunking the course on God's grace and becoming a real stinker who'll get a lot of others disgruntled.

Take good care of a brother, that he not be a whoring compromiser like Esau, who for one good bellyful surrendered his whole inheritance. For you know that later, when he wanted to be included in the family estate, he lost out and never did find a way of changing the situation, even though he tried to do so with tears in his eyes.

18. Now you all are not faced with a physical Sinai, with its crackling lightning and blackness and dense clouds and hurricane and blast of a siren and a sound of talking that made those listening beg that not one more word be said. They couldn't take an order such as, "Even if an animal should touch the mountain, it shall be stoned." To tell the truth, Moses himself was so afraid of the amazing sight that he admitted, "I'm so scared I'm shaking all over."

22. No, you all aren't faced with Mt. Sinai, but with Mt. Zion, and the city of the ever-living God, the spiritual Jerusalem. You are members of a vast body of kindred spirits, of a Church of regenerated people who have been enrolled in the spiritual order. You stand before God, Judge of all, and a jury of upright souls who have reached maturity. You are facing Jesus, the initiator of a new constitution written in blood that speaks far more eloquently than that of Abel's.

25. Be sure you don't excuse yourselves from God's sermons. For if those who excused themselves from the warnings of a human like Moses didn't get by with it, how much less chance will we have begging off from him who speaks straight from Heaven?

Once God's voice rocked the earth, but now he has made this promise:

"Once again I'll rock not only earth but heaven."

It is obvious that the phrase "once again" implies a previous clearing away of all that fell as having served its day, so that the things which didn't collapse might live on. Since we are the winners of a Kingdom unhurt by quakes, let's have a sharing spirit by which we might worship God acceptably in sincerity and in prayerfulness. For our God is a refining fire.

Chapter 13

1. Let your love for the brotherhood be for keeps, and don't you all ever forget to love strangers too. For by so doing some people entertain missionaries without knowing it. Keep the prisoners in mind as though you were in jail with them, and those who have been beat up as though the blows fell on your body.

4. In every way consider your marriage a precious thing, and don't let sexual intercourse be perverted. For God will pass judgment on those who go around tomcatting and having illicit relations. Don't let the desire for money dominate your life. Make do with what's on hand, for he himself has said, "Never will I abandon you or run off and leave you." That's why we can say with calm assurance:

> "The Lord is my provider;
> I shall never be ruled by fear.
> How shall a human do me in?"

7. Remember your leaders who brought you the word of God. Watch the results of their conduct, and imitate their living by the Unseen. However, Jesus himself is the Leader—past, present, and future. So don't get carried away by all kinds of crackpot ideas. It is better to nourish your heart on grace than your body on "health foods," which bring little benefit to those who use them.

But speaking of foods, we have a table from which even preachers aren't allowed to eat. You recall that when the blood of animals is brought into the sanctuary by the bishop for cleansing of sin, the carcasses of these animals are burned up, uneaten, outside the enclosure. So Jesus also, in order to make the people different by his supreme sacrifice, suffered *outside* the city gate. Therefore let's go out to him *outside* the restricting enclosure and accept his "excommunication". For right now, we just don't have a "city" to live in, but we're working for one that's on the way. Through him, then, let's offer a sacrifice of continual praise to God. I mean by this an unashamed public confession that we are Christians. And of course you won't forget to do good and to share all you have. For these too are sacrifices acceptable to God.

17. Listen to your leaders and do what they tell you, for they lie awake at night because of their responsibility for your spiritual welfare. Make their task a joy, and not an agony that would bring you no gain.

18. Please pray for us. We are sure that our consciences are clear, because in everything we have tried to live an exemplary life. I especially urge you to do this: Pray that I may be returned to you *real soon.*

20. Now may the God of peace, who lifted up from the dead our Lord Jesus, the great shepherd of sheep and author of an eternal Constitution written in blood—may he outfit you with everything needful to do his will. May he work out his purpose in you through Jesus Christ, to whom be the credit for all time to come. Please may it be so.

22. I urge you, my brothers, to bear with this sermon, for I really have made it short. Please know that our brother **Timothy** has been released. If he gets by here soon, I'll see you with him.

Remember us to all your leaders and to all the devoted. The group from Italy send their regards to you.

To all of you—grace!

THE LETTER OF JAMES
Practical religion

CHAPTER 1

Greetings from James, a slave of both God and the Lord Jesus Christ, to the whole Christian fellowship, wherever it may be scattered.

Consider it a real privilege, my brothers, when you are sur-rounded by all kinds of difficulties, because you know that when your faith is given a good workout it builds up your determination. And let your determination have that grown-up look, so that you might be mature and well-balanced, not short on anything. If you don't have enough understanding, ask for it from God, who gives liberally to everyone and without scolding, and it will sure-ly be given to you. But you must ask in complete trust, without any reservations. For the man with reservations is like an ocean wave whipped and ripped by the wind. Such a fellow should not think for one minute that he'll get *anything* from the Lord. He's a fence-straddler and inconsistent in all he does.

9. Let the underprivileged brother take pride in his improved condition, and let the rich brother be proud of being one of the underprivileged, since he, too, like a fragile blossom, will pass away. For as the sun and the scorching winds bear down and wither a plant, and its blossom falls off and its lovely appearance is gone, so it is with the well-to-do man. During his pilgrimage on earth he will be dried up.

12. Fortunate indeed is the man who doesn't yield to com-promise. For when he has come through the test he'll receive the "Trophy of Life" which God has promised to those who love him. Let no one in a compromised position say: "God put me in this dilemma," for God himself never makes any compromise with evil, and *never* puts anyone else in that position. The truth is that each person is dragged and pulled into compromise by his own self-interest. And self-interest, when it gets pregnant, gives

47

birth to sin, and sin grows up and spawns death. Never forget that, my dear brothers.

17. Every good gift and every mature act of sharing is from above, streaming down from the Source of light who never flickers nor enters into an eclipse. It is his intention to bring us up on the word of Truth so that we might be sort of an example to the rest of his creatures.

19. Listen here, my dear brothers. Let every man of you be quick with his ears, slow with his tongue, and hard to get riled up, because a man's temper contributes nothing to God's cause. So scrub off every spot of filth and caked-up evil and submissively accept the transplanted word which can save your souls.

22. Become doers of the word. Don't kid yourselves by being listeners only, because if a man listens to the word and doesn't act on it, he is like a person looking at himself in a mirror—he looks himself over, walks away and then forgets what he looked like. But when one takes a good look at the mature idea of freedom, and hangs on through thick and thin, not being a wishy-washy hearer but a man of action, such a person will be really happy in his work.

26. If a fellow thinks he has religion, but can't keep from running off at the mouth, and if he has a dishonest heart, that man's religion is as dead as a doornail. The religion which God the Father considers pure and clean is to look after helpless orphans and widows and to keep one's self free from the taint of materialism.

CHAPTER 2

1. My brothers, never let any prejudice creep into the faith

of our glorious Lord, Jesus Christ. For if a well-dressed person in
expensive jewelry comes to your church, and then a poor fellow
in rags comes, and you go out of your way to be nice to the well-
dressed person and say to him, "Come over here and sit by me,"
and then you say to the poor man, "Stand over there, or go up
in the balcony," don't you make distinctions in the fellowship and
become parties to vicious prejudices? Listen here, my dear brothers, hasn't God chosen the poor in this world's goods to be rich
in faith and to be full citizens in the spiritual order which he
established for those who love him? And here you go insulting the
poor! Isn't it the *rich* who oppress you and actually drag you
into court? Aren't they the ones who poke fun at the noble Name
you bear?

8. So if you observe the Scripture's finest law—"Love your
neighbor as yourself"—you're doing all right. But if you segregate,
you commit a sin, and stand convicted under the law as a violator.
Furthermore, if a man obeys the whole legal code, and yet falls
down on just one point, he has busted the whole works. For the
same one who said, "Don't fornicate," also said, "Don't murder."
So if you don't fornicate but do murder you're a lawbreaker right
on. You also must talk and act like people who can be entrusted
with the rule of freedom instead of law. For there is merciless
judgment on a merciless man, and mercy is much more preferred
than judgment.

14. What's the use, my brothers, for a man to say he has belief
but doesn't have the deeds to back it up? Can his belief do him
any good? If a brother or sister is naked and lacking the material
necessities of life, and any one of you say to them, "God bless
you. May you be warm and well fed," and yet you do nothing to
meet their physical needs, what good is it? So belief, if it is not
backed up by deeds, is dead through and through.

16. But somebody will say, "You have belief, while I have deeds." All right, show me your belief without deeds, and I will show you my belief transformed into deeds. Do you believe there's only one God? That's fine. Demons believe this too and shudder at the thought of it.

18. Do you want me to prove to you, you stubborn fellow, that belief without deeds is empty? All right, didn't our father Abraham win approval of God when he offered his son Isaac on the altar? Here you can see how his belief was helping along his deed, and how by his actions his belief was brought to maturity. It is just like the Scripture says, "So Abraham put his trust in God, since he, being a friend of God, thought it was the only right thing to do." You see, then, that a man is made whole by what he does, not merely by what he believes. Wasn't this true even of Rahab the whore? Wasn't she spared because of what she did in sheltering our spies and letting them escape by another route? So then, as the body without a spirit is dead, even so belief without deeds is dead.

CHAPTER 3

1. Many of you should stop trying to be Bible explainers, my brothers, especially since you know that we bear a much greater responsibility, and we all frequently stumble.

2. If a person is never loose-mouthed, he is a mature man, capable of exercising complete control over himself. For example, by putting a bit in a horse's mouth to control him, we are able to steer his whole body. And take a ship that's ever so big and is driven by enormous engines, yet the captain steers it wherever he wants it to go by a little biddy rudder.

5. The same is true of the tongue. It is a small organ with im-

mense potential. Just think what a roaring fire can be kindled
with a tiny match! The tongue, too, is a a flame, setting the world
afire with mischief. It has established itself among our organs and
messed up the whole body. It is hell's blowtorch, making life an
inferno. Man can tame—or has tamed—every kind of animal,
bird, reptile, and even inhabitants of the sea, yet he is unable to
control his own tongue. It is an unsubdued evil, full of deadly
poison. With it we praise the Lord and Father, and with the same
tongue we cuss out our fellow men who are made in the image
of God. From the same mouth comes a prayer and a curse. Such
a thing my brothers, should *never* be. Can good water and brack-
ish water come out of the same spring? Can a fig tree bear
peaches, my brothers, or a vine yield figs? Nor can a salt hole
give fresh water.

13. Let him who is wise and intelligent among you demonstrate, with true discipline of mind, the fruits of a noble life. But
it is nothing to be proud of when you all have bitter jealousy and
self-interest in your hearts, turning the truth into a lie. This is by
no means divine wisdom; rather it is humanistic, purely intellec-
tual, and devilish. For wherever you find jealousy and self-interest, you also find lack of discipline and every kind of false
deed. But divine wisdom is above all saintly, then peaceable, considerate, open-minded, extremely charitable and gracious, con-
sistent, unhypocritical. For the harvest of genuine peace must
first be planted by men who live it.

CHAPTER 4

1. Where does all fighting and bickering come from? Honestly
now, doesn't it arise from your mad desires for pleasure which
are literally tearing your group to pieces? You grab for everything and get nothing; you are so envious you even murder, and

still you can't be satisfied. You scrap and fight like cats and dogs. You get nothing because you haven't learned to ask for it. Even when you do ask, you don't get anything because you ask with a bad motive—so you can spend it on your own selfish pleasures. You whores, don't you know that to flirt with the world is to jilt God? Anybody who decides to run around with the world makes it clear that he is not God's friend. Or do you think that there's nothing to that Scripture which says: "He deeply yearns over the spirit he implanted in you"? What greater favor could he bestow on you? It says further: "God is against the high and mighty and is on the side of the little man." So turn yourselves over to God. Put up a fight against the devil, and he'll run from you. Walk close to God, and he'll walk close to you. Wash your hands, sinners, and clarify your motives, you two-faced people. Learn to take it on the chin, to be actively concerned and serious. Let your gaiety be changed into serious purpose, and your outward joy into solemn intent.

11. Don't run down one another, brothers. Anybody who belittles his brother or passes sentence on him actually belittles and passes sentence on God's word. And if you sit in judgment on God's word, you aren't obeying it but criticizing it. The only one who has the right to establish and pass sentence on God's word is he who has the power over life and death. So who do you think you are, you criticizer?

13. Hold on a minute now, you who talk so big and say, "Today or tomorrow we'll go to such and such a city and stay there a year buying and selling and making a killing." You don't know one blessed thing about tomorrow, or even if you'll be alive. You are just a wisp of smoke which is seen for a little while and then disappears. Instead, you should say, "If the Lord so wills we shall live and shall do this or that." But still you are proud of your big talk. All such strutting is downright wicked. And it is a sin for a man to know what is right and then not do it.

CHAPTER 5

1. And you rich guys, hold on a minute. Get ready to moan and groan because of the hardships coming on you. Your gadgets are all broken down and your pretty clothes are full of holes. Your stocks and bonds are worthless, and their certificates shall be evidence against you and will gnaw at your hearts like a flame. You piled them up for the Judgment Day.

4. Now listen, the wages of the workers who tilled your plantations and whom you cheated are crying out, and the pitiful pleas of your laborers have been heard by the Lord of Redress. You've gorged at the posh restaurants and whooped it up at the swank hotels. You've fattened yourselves like a slaughterhouse steer. You arrest and kill even an innocent person who offers no resistance.

7. But you, brothers of mine, hold on till the Lord's movement gets going. Look how the farmer awaits the precious harvest of his land, staying by it until it receives both spring and summer rains. You, too, hold on and pep your hearts, because the Lord's movement is right here. Don't gripe about one another, brothers, so as not to be convicted yourselves. Look, the Judge is ready to convene court!

10. Brothers, if you want a good example of holding on under terrific abuse, take the prophets who spoke up for the Lord. Look how we praise them for sticking it out! You've heard of Job's perseverance, and you see how the Lord brought him through, because the Lord is tenderhearted and sympathetic.

12. Above all else, brothers, don't pledge, either by the heaven or the land or by any other security. Give an honest and simple "Yes" or "No," and thus avoid condemnation.

13. If any one of you is suffering abuse, let him pray. If anyone is happy, let him sing. If one of you is sick, let him send for the church leaders, and let them pray for him and wait on him in the name of the Lord. Faithful devotion will restore the sick man, and the Lord will make well. And if he has done some sin, this too shall be forgiven him.

16. Be honest with one another about your sins, and pray for each other that you might get the victory over them, for the petition of a truly good man is powerfully effective. Elijah, for instance, was a human being just like us, and he earnestly prayed that it might not rain, and not a drop fell for three-and-a-half years. Then he prayed again and it poured, and things began to grow again.

19. My brothers, if one of you should stray from the truth, and another guides him back, you may be sure that he who guides an erring one away from his false course, will literally save his life and shield him from a lot of sins.

I, II PETER
Letters from Rock

I ROCK (Peter)

Chapter 1

1. Rock, Jesus Christ's agent, to the migrant Christians scattered through Florida, Georgia, Oklahoma, Texas and California. With his experienced eye, Father-God handpicked you and created you in his spirit, for washing and processing by Jesus Christ. May kindness and peace bust loose all over you.

3. Three cheers for the Father-God of our Lord Jesus Christ! By his overflowing mercy he has refathered us into a life of hope, based on the raising of Jesus Christ from the dead. This put us in a family that's unbroken, uncorrupted and undwindling—a spiritual family set up especially for you who are sheltered by God's power. This power is yours because of your faith in the solution that's ready to be made crystal clear at the last roundup. Delight in this, even though for a while it is necessary for you to put up with all kinds of harassment. When your faith is tested like this, it is more valuable than perishable gold which also is tested by fire. And at a time when Jesus Christ is clearly present, your faith stands out with commendation, genuineness and respect. You are indescribably happy with One whom you've never seen but still love, whom you've never caught a glimpse of, but still have faith to live by. As a result of a faith like that you'll find the answer to your deepest needs. In fact, this is the solution that was sought after and studied over by the old-time preachers who foresaw the undeserved favor that would fall on you. Under the leadership of the spirit of Christ that was in them, they studied hard to find out who would have the credentials of the suffering Christ and when he would appear. And it was made clear to them that the matters they were dealing with were not for them but for you. These very things are now explained to you by those who, in the Holy Spirit from on high, brought the Good

News to you. They are things of which angels themselves have a craving to be a part.

13. So, put work clothes on your mind and get moving. Have a grown man's hope in the spiritual power that's delivered to you at a time when Jesus Christ is clearly present. Now that you are God's obedient children, don't be controlled by the hankering you had before you saw the light. Instead, you should be different in your whole manner of life, just as he who invited you to it is different. For there's a verse which says, "You all be different, because *I* am different."

17. And if you claim as Father the One who utterly disregards a man's race and is concerned only with the way he acts, then carry out your Christian commitment with fear and trembling. Realize that you were snatched from the emptiness of your traditional ways not by material things—money and jewelry and such stuff—but by the priceless lifeblood of Christ himself, who was as innocent and harmless as a lamb. That he would do this was known from time immemorial, but it came through sharp and clear only recently when you put your trust in God who raised him from the dead and qualified him. That's why your faith and hope are rooted in God.

22. Now that by your response to the truth you have dedicated your inner lives to genuine brother-love, go ahead and love one another straight from the heart with all you've got. For you all have been refathered, not by a mortal man, but by the immortal word of a living and abiding God.

> "Every human being is like a blade of grass,
> And his appearance is like a blossom.
> The grass dries up, the blossom falls off;
> But the Word of the Lord lives on and on."

Now "the Word" is the Gospel message that was preached to you.

CHAPTER 2

1. So, then, sweep your house clean of all meanness and fibbing and double-dealing and green-eyedness and all cattiness. Like new babies, yell for the pure Gospel milk that's just right, so that you might get fat and healthy on it. When you got your first taste you saw that the Lord is real nourishing.

4. Gather around him, a live stone which the world architects considered worthless but which God prized as a jewel. And as live stones yourselves, be laid up together into a chapel for the sacred ministry of making acceptable spiritual sacrifices to God through Jesus Christ. For there's a verse like this:

> "Look, I'm laying up a stone in America,
> A prized jewel of a cornerstone;
> And the man who rests his weight on it
> won't be let down."

Its true worth, then, is for you who rest your weight on it. But for those who don't, this applies:

> "The very stone which the architects threw away has
> itself become the key stone."

Also,

> "It's a stone to stump one's toe on, a rock to trip over."

The unconvinced stump their toe on the Word. It's just their luck. But you all are a special breed, a noble clergy, a different race, a show-stock people, so that you might demonstrate the virtues of the One who called you out of darkness into his dazzling light. "The former nobodies are now God's somebodies; the outcasts are now included in the family."

11. Dear ones, I urge you as migrants and transients in a foreign land, to put the brakes on animal passions which tear you to pieces on the inside. Let your manner of life before non-Christians be so good that while they rip into you as criminals they will also get an eyeful of your fine conduct and will give the credit to God on inspection day.

13. Be loyal to anything created by the Lord for the human situation, whether it's to a king as supreme ruler or to governors as his appointees to punish criminals and to encourage the law-abiding. Such indeed is the will of God, that the law-abiding should put the muzzle on the stupid charges of half-baked people. You are free men, but only as you are God's slaves. You must not use your freedom as a disguise for evil. Hold all in honor, love the church community, give God glory, respect the King.

18. Employees, with all humility be loyal to your bosses, not only to the kind and considerate but even to the ornery ones. When someone with a God-touched conscience endures the pain of undeserved injury, this indeed is commendable. Now if you take it when you get cussed out for doing something wrong, what's so great about that? But if you're doing your job and then put up with abuse, this wins God's approval. That's why God chose you. For Christ too suffered for you and set an example for you so you might walk in his tracks. He never did a mean thing, and nobody ever caught him in a lie. When folks cussed him out, he never cussed back; when beat up, he shouted no threats; instead, he put it all in the hands of Him who sets things right. In order that we might shuck off our sins and live a good life, he bore our wrongs on his own shoulders as he hung from the tree. At his flogging you were cured. For you all were wandering aimlessly like sheep, but now you have been corralled by the shepherd and overseer of your hearts.

CHAPTER 3

1. By the same token, ladies, be loyal to your own man, so that even those who are not Christians, when they notice how nobly and humbly you live, will be won over without an argument by the exemplary life of their wives. Don't let your good looks depend on external things, like fancy hairdos, expensive jewelry and fashionable clothes, but on the inner radiance of a gentle and sweet spirit which does not fade with age. In God's eyes, this is true beauty. This is exactly the way the saintly women of old who trusted God and were loyal to their men made themselves pretty. Sarah, for instance, yielded herself completely to Abraham and spoke of him as her head. And you are true daughters of Sarah when you do the right thing and are not afraid of just any bugbear.

7. Along the same line, men, conduct your marriage with intelligence. Hold in high esteem your partners of the weaker sex, since they also are joint heirs of the life of grace; otherwise, your prayers won't reach the ceiling.

8. The whole thing in a nutshell is that you all be agreeable, sympathetic, brotherly, amiable, humble-minded, not paying back wrong for wrong or insult for insult. Instead, you all cool it, because that's why you were converted—to show that the Lord treats you real cool.

> "Anybody who wants to enjoy life,
>   And live a long time,
>   Should not let his tongue say a mean thing

Or his lips tell a lie.
He should put the brakes on badness,
   And give the throttle to goodness.
He should seek for peace and go all out after it.
For the Lord keeps an eye on the truly good,
   And a keen ear toward their prayers.
But for the wicked he has only a frown."

13. Indeed, who can hurt you if you become fireballs for good? But even if you should get pushed around for what's right —wonderful! Just don't be scared of what they're scared of, and don't get all upset. Instead, consecrate your hearts wholly to Christ the Lord, being ready at the drop of a hat to give a full explanation of your inner hope to anyone making an inquiry of you. Yet do so with gentleness and respect, keeping a clean conscience, so that when you are attacked, the people who slander the excellent way of life you have in Christ may be ashamed of themselves. For it is a sight better to get hurt for doing right, if God's will so permits it, than for doing wrong. You know that Christ, too, laid down his life once and for all for your sins—a truly just man dying for unjust men—so as to put us on the right track to God. Though his body was murdered, his spirit was made very much alive. In this state he went and preached also to the spirits in jail who, a long time ago, turned a deaf ear while God patiently called to them during the days that Noah was building the ark. A few souls—eight to be exact—were saved from the flood by the ark.

21. This flood and ark business is sort of a symbol of how baptism now saves you.* It isn't a riddance of physical filth, but a petition to God, through Jesus Christ's resurrection, for a fresh conscience. When Christ entered the spiritual realm, all angels,

---

* That is, by putting you on board the Christian "ark," or community.

rulers and the high and mighty were placed under his command, and he himself became God's righthand man.

CHAPTER 4

1. Since Christ took a beating physically, you-all, too, prepare yourselves with the same insight. It's a plain fact that anybody who takes a physical beating has broken away completely from wickedness, with the result that he no longer spends the rest of his life on earth swayed by society's expectations but by God's will. For you have already put in enough time in the past in service to the pagan world, going along with them in sex orgies, stupid cravings, beer guzzlings, wild parties, drinking sprees, and religious flings. They think you are queer now for not buddying up with them in such a flood of asininity, so they poke a lot of fun at you. Okay, they will account for every word to him who is ever on the alert to judge both the living and the dead. That's why the gospel was preached also to the dead—that they might be judged on the same basis as people who haven't died, and might live in the spirit according to God's plan.

7. The goal of everything has come upon us. So get with it and pray like you mean it. Above all, try hard to love each other, because love smooths over a pile of wrongs. Keep your latch-strings on the outside for one another, without griping about it. As responsible handlers of God's many-sided grace, serve others with whatever gift each has received. If someone has the gift of words, let him share God's words; if someone has a knack for lay service, let him throw all his God-given strength into it. In every way so live as to be a credit to God through Jesus Christ, to whom is the praise and the power throughout all ages. May it ever be so.

12. Dear ones, don't consider the bath of fire you're going through as something unusual, or that an extraordinary thing has happened to you. Instead, let the fact that you are sharing in the sufferings of Christ be a source of real joy to you. Then at the unveiling of his glory your joy will be simply out of this world. You're especially fortunate when you catch hell just because you are Christians. That's a sure sign that a beautiful spirit—God's spirit—is roosting in your heart. On the other hand, don't ever get into trouble as a murderer or a thief or a crook or a meddler in someone else's business. It's when you suffer *as a Christian* that you need never be ashamed. Praise God that you bear such a name!

17. The day of reckoning is going to start off with church people. Now if we are the first ones to be called up, what will be the final outcome of those who have turned a deaf ear to God's Good News? And if a truly good man barely squeaks by, what are the chances of a hypocrite and a scoundrel? So then, let those who are having a rough time for doing the will of God entrust their hearts fully to the faithful Creator by continuing in their good behavior.

CHAPTER 5

1. Now please let me urge you pastors, since I am your fellow pastor and an actual witness to Christ's mistreatment, and am also your partner in the dawning Christian era: Be good shepherds of the flock that God has put in your care. Do this gladly before God, and not out of a sense of duty; from the heart and not with an eye on the salary. Don't lord it over the members, but be examples for the congregation. And when the Head Shepherd arrives, he'll bestow on you an honorary degree that keeps its luster.

5. Similarly, you assistants be cooperative with the pastors. All of you should wear the jeans of gentleness, because God is dead set against the arrogant, but gives his favor to the humble. So then, bring yourselves low under the hand of Almighty God, that he may stand you on your feet at the proper time. Let him in on all your problems, because you mean much to him.

8. Sober up now, and get with it. That old roaring lion—your adversary, the Devil—is stalking around looking for someone to gobble up. Put steel in your faith and stand up to him, realizing that the brotherhood in other parts of the world is enduring the same kind of persecution. But after you have taken it for a while, the God of all kindness, who through Christ invited you into his marvelous era, will personally make you as good as new. He will make you secure and give you vigor and will undergird you. May He rule the rolling ages. Please may it be so.

12. I have dictated this little letter to you through Silas, whom I consider a reliable brother. I just wanted to spur you on and to add my testimony that this truly is God's gracious gift. Plant your feet in it.

13. The fellowship here in "the ghetto" sends you greetings, as does my son, Mark. Give each other a big hug of love. To all you Christians—Shalom.

                    Yours,
                    Rock

II ROCK (Peter)

CHAPTER 1

1. From Simon (Rock), a "captive" of Jesus Christ, as well as his agent, to those who, due to the fairness of our God and Savior Jesus Christ, have gotten a faith that's every bit as good as ours. May you have lots of undeserved favor and peace as you get to know God and our Lord Jesus better.

3. Through his divine power and through the knowledge of him who has invited us because of the goodness of his own heart, he has loaded us up with all we need for the good life. In so doing he has dealt us in on some wonderful offers that are out of this world. By accepting them you may become partners in the divine order and may escape from the awful hellishness which greed generates in the world. On top of this, you should do your dead-level best to put goodness in your faith;

> wisdom in your goodness,
> self-control in your wisdom;
> patience in your self-control,
> godliness in your patience;
> brotherliness in your godliness,
> and love in your brotherliness.

8. Being packed down and running over with these things keeps you from being duds and washouts in the course of the Lordship of Jesus Christ. But the man who hasn't got them is nearsighted and is going blind; he has become forgetful of his previous cleansing from his sins. So, brothers, concentrate all the more on taking the slack out of your Christian commitment and assignment. By doing so, you won't ever fall overboard. What's more, you'll be guaranteed full admission into the spiritual movement of our Lord and Savior, Jesus Christ.

12. Well, I'm going to keep right on nagging you on these matters, even though you are fully aware of them and have been drilled in the essential points. So, as long as I'm in this "house," I think it is a good idea to keep jogging your memory. I realize that in a little while I'll be moving out of my "house," just as our Lord Jesus Christ made clear to me. That's why I'll do my best to help you always to have a clear memory of these things even after I've checked out. For when we made known to you the power and the presence of our Lord Jesus, we didn't bait you along with polished sermons; rather, we spoke from firsthand experience of his greatness. For we were there on the holy hill with him when he accepted from Father-God honor and praise, as a voice came to him with surpassing glory. With our own two ears we heard that voice coming in from heaven and saying, "This is my dearly loved Son, of whom I'm real proud."

19. Also, we put the prophetic word on a more solid footing, and you'll do yourself a favor by clutching it as though it were a light in a dismal swamp, and hanging on to it until day breaks and "Light-bearer" rises in your hearts.

20. Understand this from the outset: No prophetic writing launches itself.* For prophecy is never produced by human volition; instead, as men get carried away by holy spirit, they speak for God.

CHAPTER 2

1. Now just as there were phony preachers among the people then, so will there be phony teachers among you too. They will

---

* Or, arises under its own impetus.

introduce false teachings that are destructive, while disowning
the Owner who paid for them and while consigning themselves
to hell in a hurry. And a lot of folks will imitate their immorality
and bring disgrace on the true way. They are so greedy they'll
whip up speeches just to get the honorariums from you. These
jerks will find that old-time judgment isn't a thing of the past and
that their doom isn't napping. For if God did not exempt angels
when they went astray, but put them in dark hellholes while
awaiting trial; and if he didn't spare the ancient world, but
slapped a flood on the whole godless business, sparing only the
eight in the ark because Noah was living right; and if God
brought catastrophe on Sodom and Gomorrah and made ashes
of them as an example of what happens to an irreligious setup;
and if he rescued a good man like Lot who was heavily burdened
by the filthy and loose behavior about him, whose tender heart
was torn day after day by the sight and sound of the immoral
acts of people he lived among; then the Lord clearly knows how to
get sincere folks out of trying situations, and how on the day of
sentencing, to dish out punishment on guilty people, especially on
those who, scorning discipline, go trotting after the corrupt cravings of the lower nature. Daring and self-willed, they insult those
in high positions without batting an eye. Why, not even angels,
though greater in strength and power, would bring such insolent
charges against them before the Lord himself.

12. But these jokers are like natural-born dumb animals that
are trapped and slaughtered. They poke fun at things they don't
even understand. As they slaughter, so shall they be slaughtered;
acting unjustly, they'll be paid with injustice. Their idea of fun is
to have a fling in broad-open daylight. Splotched and deformed,
they wallow around while deceitfully taking communion with
you. They have eyes that see nothing but sex, that are eternally
hungry for the obscene. They seduce the innocent. They are bastards who have a heart exercised in greediness. Having jumped
the straight and narrow, they highballed it to hell, taking the

same route as the Reverend Balaam Berry, who loved the money he got for doing wrong but was rebuked for his waywardness when a dumb jackass, talking like a man, prevented the preacher from making an ass of himself.

17. These kooks are dry wells, wisps of fog lashed by a hurricane, who have a reservation in the blackness of the nether regions. Running off at the mouth with a lot of poppycock, and with their uncontrolled hankering for sex, they seduce those who are on the verge of breaking away from their false standards. "Let's be free," they bark at everyone, while they themselves are slaves of destructive habits. (For to whatever a man sells out, to that is he a slave.)

20. Now, if by an understanding of the Lord and Savior Jesus Christ, people break away from the pollutions of the old order and then get entangled in them again and sell out, they are worse off at the end than at the beginning. They would have been better off never to have known the right way than to have understood it and then turned their backs on the precious truth delivered to them. This proverb describes them perfectly: "A dog will eat his vomit," and also, "A washed hog will still wallow in the mud."

Chapter 3

1. This makes the second letter, my dear ones, that I have written to you. Each time, by refreshing your memory, I have tried to clarify your mind, to keep before you the previous sermons of the saintly preachers as well as the will of the Lord and Savior as expressed by your missionaries. Keep this uppermost in your minds—that when time begins to run out, impudent mockers who run after nothing but their own interests will come and say to you: "Where is the evidence of his aliveness? For from the beginning of creation right up to the present generation things continue in the same old rut." But here's what they purposefully forget: that the heavens existed for ages and then, at God's command, the earth was formed out of water and divided by water. Again at his command, that world then was flooded and destroyed. All right, the present heavens and earth, by that same command, are being reserved for fire, and kept for the day of trial and sentencing of needless people.

8. So please don't forget, dear ones, that from God's viewpoint a single day may be the same as a thousand years, or a thousand years the same as a single day. The Lord just doesn't present his evidence according to some peoples' timetable. But he does yearn over you all, not wanting anybody to go to hell, but everybody to enter into a transformed life.

10. Now Lord's Day will slip up on you like a thief. At that time the skies will disappear with a blast, the basic elements of life will be consumed in the heat, and the entire earth will become uninhabitable. In the light of this total destruction, what kind of persons should you be? Shouldn't your life together be one of dedication and deep concern as you wait for and encourage the breaking in of God's day, on which the blazing skies will be smashed and the earth's structures will melt away in roaring flames. But, on the basis of his assurance, we live in anticipation of "a new heaven and a new earth, in which justice makes its home."

14. So then, dear ones, as you anticipate these things, do your darnedest to be clean and straight and to be found in peace with Him. Consider our Lord's perseverance in salvation, just as our beloved brother Paul wrote to you with the insight that had been granted to him. Notice how he mentioned these things in every one of his letters. To be sure, some of the things he said are really hard to understand, and people who are unlearned and flighty twist them out of shape, just as they do the other writings, to their own destruction.

17. So now that you've been given advance notice, my loved ones, really be careful not to be taken for a ride or knocked off your balance by the slick tricks of smooth operators. Rather, keep on growing in the undeserved favor and knowledge of our Lord and Savior Jesus Christ. To him be the credit both now and on the day of eternity!

Love,
Rock

I, II, III JOHN
Letters from Jack

I JACK (John)

CHAPTER 1

1. In order that you-all, too, might be our partners, we're plainly telling you about something that's real, something that we ourselves have heard, that we have seen with our own two eyes. It's about the idea of life which we looked at and even felt of with our own hands. Now the life took shape and we saw it, and we are giving you our word and plainly telling you about the spiritual life which was with the Father and which took shape in front of us. Our partnership, then, is with the Father and with his son Jesus Christ. And we are recording this so that the joy of us all may be completely full.

5. And here is the announcement which we have heard from him and are relaying to you: "God is light and there isn't a single speck of darkness in him." If we say that we are in partnership with him and keep on gadding about in the dark, we're just plain lying and not acting on the truth. But if we keep moving in the light, as he himself is in the light, we are in partnership with one another, and the sacrifice of his son Jesus Christ is ridding us of every sin. If we say, "We don't have a sin," we're kidding ourselves and are not truthful. If we honestly face up to our sins, he is so fair and straight that he will put our sins behind him and will rid us of every bad habit. If we keep saying, "We've never done anything wrong," we make a liar out of him, and his idea is not rooted in us.

CHAPTER 2

1. Children of mine, I'm writing to you like this so you won't go wrong; however, if a person does go wrong, we have a fair-minded lawyer, Jesus Christ, to represent us before the Father. He indeed is the bondsman for our misdeeds—not for ours alone but also for those of the whole world as well. And the reason we are sure that we are his client is that we act on his orders. The person who says, "I'm his client," and doesn't act on his instructions, is a phony who simply isn't telling the truth. But the person who follows his advice is the one in whom the love of God has matured. That's how we can tell if we are Christians. Anyone who claims to be a Christian is obliged to live the same life he lived.

7. Loved ones, I'm not introducing a *new* instruction to you, but an *old* one which you've had all along. The old instruction is the message you listened to. And yet, it is a new instruction that I'm writing about, and it's true both in his experience and yours, that the darkness is lifting and the true light is already dawning. Now a man who claims to be in the light, but still hates his brother is in the darkness right on. The man who loves his brother lives in the light and has no trick up his sleeve. But he who hates his brother is in the dark, lives in the dark and has no idea what direction he's going, because the darkness has blindfolded him.

12. I'm writing to you, children, because your misdeeds through his name, are being forgiven. I'm writing to you adults, because you know the Source. I'm writing to you young people, because you have conquered the Devil. I write to you, children, because you know the Father. I write to you, fathers, because you know the Source. I write to you, young people, because you are strong, and God's Idea lives in you and you have conquered the Devil.

15. Don't love the old order or the things which keep it going. If anyone loves the old order, it is not the Father's love that's in him. For everything that's in the old order—the hankering for physical comforts, the hankering for material things, the em-

I JOHN

phasis on status—is not from the Father but is from the old order
itself. And the old order, with its hankerings, is collapsing, but
he who lives by the will of God moves into the New Age.

18. Children of mine, it's real late. Just as you were advised
that a Christ-fighter is coming, so now they are all over the place!
That's how we know that it's *real late*. They came from our midst,
all right, but they never were genuinely one with us, because if
they had been they would have stuck with us. By leaving, they
proved that not all of us are sincere.

20. Now you all have a special insight from the Holy One
and you are fully aware of it. I did not write to you that you do
not know the truth, but that you *do* know it, and that nothing
phony ever springs from the truth. Who really is the phony, if it
isn't the one who denies Jesus' authority? He indeed is the Christ-
fighter, the rejecter of both Father and Son. Anybody who re-
jects the prince has no loyalty to the king. Anybody who openly
supports the prince is also loyal to the king. As for you all, follow
your original instructions. If you do so, you'll follow both Son
and Father. And the guarantee which he himself has made to us
is spiritual life.

26. I wrote to you along these lines about those who are hood-
winking you. Now, you-all, the special insight which you received
from him is still in you and you don't need anybody to teach
you. Moreover, just as his special insight, which is genuine and
not a sham, gives you guidance on all matters, even so stick with
him just as he taught you.

28. And now, my little ones, stick with him, so that whenever
he appears we can look him in the eye and not hang our heads
in shame before him on his triumphal day. If you are convinced
that he is just, you may be sure that a man of justice is his offspring.

77

CHAPTER 3

1. Just imagine how much love the Father showed us by allowing us to be called "children of God." And that's exactly who we are. The reason that the old order doesn't understand us is that it didn't understand him. My loved ones, at present we are "children of God," though our future has not yet taken shape. We do know that when it does take shape we'll be just like him, that we shall see him exactly as he is. And everyone who so pins his hope on him dedicates himself, just as Christ himself is dedicated.

4. The person who practices wrong also practices disobedience, since wrong is disobedience. And you are aware that Christ was given that he might remove wrongs, even as there is no wrong in him. Any person who sticks with him doesn't wallow around in sin. The man who wallows in sin hasn't taken a good look at him nor clearly understood him.

7. My children, don't let anybody pull the wool over your eyes: He who practices justice is just even as Christ himself is just. And he who practices evil is devil-inspired, because from the start the Devil practices evil. For this very reason the Son of God was born that he might break up the Devil's doings. Anyone who has been fathered by God doesn't make wrong a habit, because he carries in him his Father's genes. Since God has fathered him he just can't wallow in sin. That's how God's offspring are distinguished from the Devil's offspring. Any person who doesn't practice justice and who doesn't love his brother is not fathered by God. For the word you got from the start is this: "Let us love one another." We are not to be like Cain whose father was the Evil One and who murdered his brother. And *why* did he murder him? Because his ways were wicked and his brother's ways were right.

13. So don't be surprised, brothers, if the old order hates your guts. We ourselves are convinced that we have switched from death to life because we love the brothers. The man with no love still lives in death country. The brother-hater is a man-killer, and you know that no man-killer has spiritual life residing in him.

16. Christ laid down his life for us and taught us what love really is. So we too should lay down our lives for the brothers. Now if somebody who has material things sees his brother in need and then padlocks his concern for him, how does the love of God stay in him? My little ones, let's not *talk* about love. Let's not *sing* about love. Let's put love into *action* and make it *real*. By so doing we'll know that we are truth-people and shall bolster our conscience before God. And even if our conscience still hurts us, God is bigger than our conscience and knows every detail.

21. My loved ones, if our conscience doesn't hurt us, we feel at ease around God. Then, if we ask something of God, we start receiving because we are acting on his instructions and are carrying out his wishes. And his instruction to us is this: Live up to the name of his Son Jesus Christ and love one another, just as he told us to do. The person who faithfully follows his instructions keeps company with God and God keeps company with him. And the reason we know that he keeps company with us is that he shared his spirit with us.

CHAPTER 4

1. Dear ones, don't fall for just any religious person that comes along. Instead, give religious people a thorough road test to see if God actually sent them, because a lot of phony preachers have descended on the world. Here's the way you recognize God's spiritual man: Every one who takes his stand on the humanity of Jesus Christ is rooted in God. And every one who does not so take his stand on Jesus is not rooted in God. And the latter is from the Christ-fighter, about whose coming you were advised and who is already in the world right now. But you-all, my little ones, being rooted in God, have gotten the upper hand over them, because the One who moves in you is greater than the one who moves in the old order. They indeed are part and parcel of the old order. Accordingly, they speak on behalf of the old order and those in the old order respond to them. We, however, are rooted in God, and the person who is sensitive to God responds to us, while the one who is not rooted in God does not respond to us. In this way we distinguish the spirit of the truly sincere person from the spirit of the hypocrite.

7. Loved ones, let's love each other, because love springs from God, and every lover has been fathered by God and is sensitive to God. The nonlover is not sensitive to God because God *is* love. And God's love took shape in our midst when he sent his one and only son into the world so we might start living. And that's real love—not that we loved God, but that he loved us and sent his son to answer for our wrongs. Loved ones, if God loved *us* that much, then *we* ought to love one another. Nobody has ever once caught a glimpse of God. Yet if we love everybody, God is present among us and his love is brought to maturity in us.

13. The fact that he gave us his spirit assures us that we are in unity with him and he with us. And we ourselves have both experienced and are the evidence that the Father has sent his son to be mankind's deliverer. Whenever one takes his stand on the fact that Jesus is God's son, God is present in him and he in God. So we have both experienced, and based our lives on, the love that God has put in us.

16. God is love, and the person who stays in love stays in God, and God stays in him. In this way love has made men of us, so that in the time of crisis we may have guts. For just as he faced the world, so do we. Fear and love don't mix; mature love actually expels fear. Since fear clips a man's wings, he who fears has not yet matured in love.

19. Because he first loved us, we ourselves are practicing love. If someone says, "I love God," and is hating his brother, he is a phony. For the man who has no love for his visible brother cannot possibly have love for the invisible God. So the advice we get from him is that the God-lover is also a brother-lover.

CHAPTER 5

1. Everyone who recognizes that Jesus is the rightful ruler has been fathered by God. Now if one loves the father, one also loves the father's child. By the same token, when we love God and do what he tells us, we can be sure that we also love God's children. To love God is to follow his instructions, and his instructions are not unreasonable, since the true child of God wins hands down over the old order. And it is our way of life that licks the old order. Who is it that licks the old order if it isn't the one who bases his life on Jesus as God's son?

6. This same Jesus Christ came in body and mind—not in body only but in both body and mind; the spirit also is evidence, because the spirit is the real thing. There are, then, three convincing factors—the soul, the body, and the mind, and the three make a whole.*

If we accept evidence presented by people, God's evidence is even greater, because this *is* God's evidence which he presented concerning his son. The person who bases his life on the son of

---

* This passage, verses 6-8, is very difficult to interpret and translate into modern equivalents. Literally, it says: "This is the one who came by means of water and blood—Jesus Christ. Not in the water only but in the water and

God has the evidence within himself. He who does not base his life on God has already made God a phony because he has not acted on the evidence which God presented concerning his son. And the evidence is this: That God gave us spiritual life and this life is in his Son. Who has the Son has the life; who has not the Son of God has not the life.

13. I wrote all this to you who live up to the name of the Son of God, so as to assure you that you have spiritual life. And the thing that puts us at ease around him is that when we ask for something in line with his purpose he really listens to us. And if we are sure that he listens to us when we present a need, we are sure that we get responses from him to what we proposed.

---

in the blood. And the spirit [or breath] is the evidence, because the spirit [or breath] is the truth. There are three facts of evidence, the spirit [breath] and the water and the blood, and the three are in one." The key words, of course, are "water," "blood," and "spirit." Almost without exception, the translators and commentators that I have consulted interpret "water" as Jesus' baptism, "blood" as his death, and "spirit" as the Holy Spirit. I cannot accept this interpretation for the simple reason that it doesn't make sense. Jesus did not come by, in, or through his baptism or his death. And certainly his baptism, his death and the Holy Spirit are not one or in one.

I suggest, then, that "water" refers to the primary element out of which the Hebrews believed the earth to have been formed. In the story of creation "the earth was without form, and void; and darkness was upon the face of the deep. And the Spirit of God moved upon the face of the waters" (Gen.1:2 KJV). Peter speaks of earth as "formed out of water and by means of water." (II Peter 3:5 RSV) So like the rest of all the physical creation, Jesus came through "water," the primordial substance of all things created. He had a form, a *physical body.*

But John insists that Jesus came not through water alone—that he was not merely matter or body—but also through "blood." Since the ancients believed that the blood was the container of life, and that it distinguished animate from inanimate matter, perhaps blood here refers to Jesus' animate (cf. "animal") nature with a mind or intelligence. He was a live, "blooded" being, with "animus," or mentality.

Yet having form, or substance, and physical rational life, or blood, isn't enough. He has "spirit" or breath. (The Greek word is the same for both.) When the Lord God formed man he "breathed into his nostrils the breath of life; and man became a living soul." (Gen. 2:7 KJV). This breath, or soul, is the very essence of man, or as John puts it, "the soul is the truth," the reality (verse 6). So these three—the "water," the "blood," the "breath" (or as we would put it, the body, mind, and soul) —are the three evidences of the one whole, the fully human son of God.

16. If someone sees his brother engaging in sin, but not to the point of death, he shall pray for him and God will give him life. But this is not for those sinning to death. There is such a thing as sinning to the point of death. I'm not saying that you should pray about that. All wickedness is sin, but there is such a thing as sin not to the point of death.

18. We are aware that anyone who has been fathered by God does not wallow in sin; instead the one who has been fathered by God holds on to him and the evil one doesn't run off with him. We're convinced that our life is from God, and that the whole old order is in cahoots with the devil. We're sure that God's son has come, and has given us the ability to recognize the true One. And we are in the true One, in his Son Jesus Christ. This indeed is the true God and spiritual life. So, my little ones, don't let false gods sweep you off your feet.

Yours,
Jack

II JACK (John)

1. From the pastor, to the official board and to all whom it represents. I truly love you-all. And not just I, but all the others who know what truth is. They do so because of the truth that's living in us and will always be with us. May there be on all of us favor and compassion and peace from Father-God and from Jesus Christ, who in truth and in love is the Father's Son.

4. I'm extremely happy to find those of your membership walking in truth, just as we were told by the Father. And now I am urging you, the official board, "let's *love* one another." (I'm not writing to you as though this were a fresh exhortation, but one which we've had all along.) And love means that we are to follow his instructions. The specific order, just as you recall from the very start, is that you walk in love.

7. A lot of quacks—people who deny the full humanity of Jesus—are footloose in the world. Such a person is indeed both a quack and a Christ-fighter. Give him a wide berth so you won't flunk out on the training we've given you but will come through with flying colors.

9. The man who is so liberal he doesn't stick with Christian teaching has no God. He who sticks with the teaching has both the Father and the Son. If some guy comes along who doesn't uphold this teaching, give him neither hospitality nor encouragement. Anybody who encourages him is a partner with him in his erroneous ways.

12. I have a lot of things to write to you-all, but I won't try to put them on paper. Instead, I'm hoping to get by your way so we can talk face to face. That'll make us all happy.

13. The members of the official board of your sister church   .
ask to be remembered to you.

Yours,   ·
Jack

III JACK (John)

1. From the pastor, to beloved Gayle, whom I truly love.

2. My dear one, above all else I pray that you are doing well and are in good health, the same as you are doing spiritually. For I was mighty happy when some brothers got here with news about your truth-life and how committed you are to it. Nothing pleases me more than to hear that my chillun are walking in the truth.

5. My loved one, you're really on the beam when you lend a hand to the brothers, even though they may be strangers to you. They spoke about your love at the church meeting. It's wonderful when you chip in on their expenses so they can travel like men of God. For they launched out for Christ without taking one dime from outsiders. That's why *we* ought to get in the harness with such people, that we all might be partners in the truth.

9. I wrote to the church about a matter, but Godbold, who loves to be their big wheel, doesn't pay us any mind. So when I get there, I'll review his record of insolent mouthings against us. And as if this weren't enough, he not only pays no mind to the brothers himself, but he threatens those who do want to, and turns them out of the church.

11. My dear brother, don't copy evil but good. The man who does good is God's man; the man who does evil has had no vision of God.

12. People from all over surely do speak highly of Doug Smith; indeed, the facts speak for themselves. And we're glad to add our word to this, and our word, you know, is sincere.

13. I have a lot of things to write to you about, but I'll not try it on *this* typewriter. I'm still hoping to see you shortly and we'll chew the fat then. The friends here send you their love. Give our personal regards to the friends there.

Sincerely,
Jack

JUDE
A letter from Joe

JOE (Jude)

1. From Joe, Jim's brother, and owned by Jesus Christ lock, stock, and barrel; to the church members—people who have been loved by Father-God and nursed by Jesus Christ. May you all be loaded up with kindness and peace and love.

3. My dear ones, while doing my dead-level best to write to you about our mutual salvation I had the urge to get a letter off to you begging you to fight like fury for the way of life that has been totally entrusted to the Christians. For some guys have come into the church like snakes in the grass. (It was pointed out in earlier writings that they would stoop to this.) They are uncommitted; they twist the undeserved favor of our God into a cover-up for their lewdness; and they disown Jesus Christ as our only ruler and master.

5. I'd like to refresh your memory a bit on some things you're already thoroughly familiar with: (1) that while on the first time around God *delivered* the people from Egypt, on the second he *destroyed* those who didn't live their faith; (2) that He has kept in the hole, without bail, for sentencing on the Great Day, those missionaries who didn't stick to their assignment but ran away from their own stations; (3) that London and Berlin and their suburbs, acting in the same way, went whoring and trekking off after some stranger, and they serve as a perfect example of piling up a punishment of consuming fire.

8. And so it is with these fellows I'm warning you about. With their imaginations they debase the human body; they utterly disregard leaders, and they snicker at sacred things. Why, not even Michael the archangel dared poke fun at the *devil* when he was arguing with him over Moses' body. Rather, he politely said, "The Lord will tend to you." But these jerks sneer when they don't know what it's all about, and when, like dumb animals, they do catch on to something naturally, they make a joke even of that. Hell on them, because they're behaving exactly like Cain, and are rushing pellmell into the error of Balaam who preached for pay; and in an uprising like Korah's they are being destroyed. These people are a disgrace at your church suppers, brazenly coming to the table while interested in nobody but themselves. They are rainless cloud-puffs scurrying in the breeze. They are trees at harvesttime with nothing on them, dead as a doornail, pulled up by the roots. They are tempestuous waves of the sea, boiling up their own shameful froth. They are off-course stars, doomed to the eternal outer darkness.

14. Now Enoch, who lived in the seventh generation after Adam, was clearly referring to these people when he said, "Look here, the Lord appeared with a vast throng of his followers to create a time of crisis for all people and to convince all the insolent of the insolent acts they have committed against him, and of all the brazen things they have hurled in his teeth" These jokers are belly-aching gripes who do only as they pretty well please. They are windbags who lick boots for status.

17. But you-all, my dear, dear people, constantly bear in mind the things you were told previously by those sent out by our Lord Jesus Christ. They told you, "When time runs out there will be men who make a joke of their religion and follow their own insolent desires." These are the segregationists-kooks without a conscience. But you, my loved ones, deepen your commitment to your most sacred way of life. With spirit-filled prayer keep yourselves in God's love. Always be eager for the kindness of our Lord Jesus Christ which leads into spiritual life.

22. You must deal gently with some people who are wavering but others you are to save by actually snatching them from the fire. Still others you must handle with gloves, as much as you may dislike their clothing messed up by their own filth.

24. Now to him who can keep you on your feet and present you at his court, spick-and-span and happy, to the only God, our Savior, through Jesus Christ our Lord, be glory, greatness, power and pre-eminence throughout the past, present and future.

Sincerely,
Joe